Build Me a Boat

Words for Music 1968-2018

Books by Michael Dennis Browne

The Wife of Winter
Sun Exercises
The Sun Fetcher
Smoke from the Fires
Selected Poems 1965-1995
Give Her the River
You Won't Remember This
Things I Can't Tell You
Panthers
What the Poem Wants: Prose on Poems
The Voices
Chimes

Build Me a Boat

Words for Music 1968-2018

Michael Dennis Browne

Carnegie Mellon University Press
Pittsburgh 2020

Acknowledgments

A deep bow to all the musicians (composers, conductors, singers, instrumentalists) who have—so memorably, so variously—brought these words to life.

Gratitude to all the publishers from over the years for permission to reproduce these words.

Special thanks to Gerald Costanzo and Cynthia Lamb at Carnegie Mellon University Press for exceptional support.

The cover art is an illustration by Donal Mac Polin from his book *The Drontheim: Forgotten Sailing Boat of the North Irish Coast*.

Book design by Connie Amoroso

Library of Congress Control Number 2020939493
ISBN 978-0-88748-658-6
Copyright @ 2020 by Michael Dennis Browne
All rights reserved
Printed and bound in the United States of America

10   9   8   7   6   5   4   3   2   1

for Eddie and Paddy

"O the rising of the sun
And the running of the deer
The playing of the merry organ
Sweet singing in the choir"

Contents

1

2

3

4

5

6

1

All My Pretty Ones

in loving memory of Anne Sexton
(for soprano and piano)

1/ In a Tree at Dawn to Listen to Birds

I had wanted to hide.
I had wanted to stay there and hear
the whole day's songs.

I who am not satisfied
with my speech,
so heavy, so human,
I had wanted to learn their lightness.

I who am not pleased
with my name,
I had hoped they would think me
their fellow among the green
and fling me a new one.

When I had climbed back down
to where I belong,
among women, among men,
the singing began again.

2/ And the Birds Arrive

And the birds arrive.
It means it is morning,
it means it is day.
The night tree shakes them out.
This is a life lived alone.

This is a life lived like a tree.

This tree waits for its birds.

I don't remember the dream.
I keep the image of a courtyard.
I have lost my people of the dream.

Now my dawn company has come.
The guests, for feeding.
It means it is morning.
It means it is day.

Still I want the dream, the delicate.
There I fly to feed.
I have lost my people of the dream.

And the birds arrive.
As sons, as daughters, they will do.
They sing the light into change
among sunflower, cracked corn.
For light alone they sing,
the feeders sway.

It means it is morning,
it means it is day.

3/ Purple Finch

A finch with a broken neck lies by my house.
I must assume the coroner of birds would say
the neck was broken.
I suppose he flew against my window.
I take the sharp spade and dig
through the first snow. The ground

is not yet frozen, but hardening.
I dig through a thick root.
I dig past where the dogs would reach,
who are watching.
I dig through the old worlds,
where the worms still rule.
I dig past the gates and exits of that.
I dig through five kinds of color,
I dig through gold and blue and scarlet and black and green.
I dig past color.
I dig till I feel I have reached
air again,
air of a quieter kind,
where he can ride
in a time of waiting.
With a mind for all who descend,
I lower the broken bird.

4/ Feeder

The same day I build
a feeder for the winter birds,
two grosbeaks, male and female,
are feeding there.
His chest is yellow, bright,
hers milder, a kind of gray.
The feeder is fixed to a bare tree,
whose leaves these birds become,
female and male leaves,
both bright and mild.

5/ Little Life

Life,
O little life,
what is happening to you?

You one among many,
don't you like to be
just a tree of the wood?

O little life,
let the birds come down
on you,

let them sing
above your speech,
which should diminish,

let the rains wet
you, let storms shake
you—and shine with your storm.

The earth lies deep
where your roots grip—
and your arms in air—

she guards the seeds
of space in her;
you are feeding there.

Life,
O little life,
it is happening to you.

6/ The Bird Inside

And when I am calm
the bird arrives inside.
Who slows between the eyes.
Who spreads long wings.

This is she and he of the center.
Wing Shadow. Wing Light.
And stands. And stands.
Without memory. Without desire.

Who comes when I am calm.
Who stands at the center.
Who does not feed, nor sing.
Without memory. Without desire.

Who grows. Till the skull fill,
till all my head be bird,
bird-bones be mine, and I rise.
Without memory. Without desire.

7/ Night Bird

I know what the night bird wants

choose   choose   choose   choose
      easy   easy   easy   easy

just under tongues
the night bird lives

night bird among the leaves

she has wings enough
for everyone
there is milk enough
in that breast for feeding

choose   choose   choose   choose
     easy   easy   easy   easy

she has a new name in mind
each to receive the new name
hidden just under
hidden just under
the old one
who out there, but near
who nearer
who nearer
now now now now
   in   in   in   in

O Mother of Bones
Mother of Names

I know what the night bird wants.

8/ All My Pretty Ones

Do you see? There!
It is the grosbeak   it is the chickadee
come to crack
seeds, seeds I have set out
it is the purple finch   it is the gold

All my pretty
        all my pretty
                all my pretty ones

return

Do you hear? There!
thrum! thrum!
wind of their wings
some singly   some paired
some with their tribe
some with a quick, a silvery
some with a slower singing

All my pretty
        all my pretty
                all my pretty ones

return

I had forgotten
I had feared to wake to songs
which ask that all of the heart be used

How many dyings
and still this singing
no question of no song
from the breast intended for singing

Do you hear? There!
in light now
        from shelter
                from sleep
it is the nuthatch   it is the sparrow
the thrush the cardinal the jay

O little life

All my pretty
              all my pretty
                           all my pretty ones
return

Mad Book, Shadow Book (Michael Morley's Songs)

(for tenor and piano)

Michael Morley Creaked

Michael Morley creaked through the midnight wood
like a grandfather clock.
All the shadows followed
as if he were raw meat.
He slid over the snow
like a skillet down a slope, he was electric!
Morley broke into an empty classroom
& took off his wheels.
He broke into a ladder full of photographs,
he set up a photograph of a ladder
against a waterfall.
He ran up the waterfall
& set the fish on fire!

Falling Asleep in the Afternoon

Again I am
falling asleep in the afternoon,
not "falling in love again" but
falling asleep in the afternoon.
The glass in the window thickens
until only the room is mine,
and then the room inside the room,
through which I begin to run.

I Feel Good Running

I feel good running
so I run and run.
I run through the wood in a hood.
I run through a pie
my mother is making in England.
I run through my brother's fingers
as he lifts his hands to his head.
And I dump & burn my winter hands.
I burn the Winter Man.
I snap Death's stream on my knee.
I am the King who had been hiding
in the tree.
I run though the ruins,
restoring the ruins as I run.

Morley's Root Song

The cat keeps bringing
birds into the house; some I save.
They are not fit for flight,
they are no use for song.
Bent birds, songs without words.
Lost between wing & wing, the knight, the rider,
doing the dark roads.

> my root is rubble & barbed wire
> my root is not sweet
> my root is army in the snow

Now in my mad book
I do read,

now in my shadow book
I do peer; all is clear
as night to me.
Every animal is sad;
sing nonny no, sing hey nonny.
Mamma Mia. Cosa Nostra. Bossa Nova.

> my root's a goat
> my root is a cellar door
> my root is bruise of jewels

The dreams I had when I was a boy
I have forgotten. Gone.
Dreaming Verboten. Going, going, gone.
E Pericoloso Sporgersi. Morley Morley Boy.
I have forgotten who I was.
Rivers run through my rooms.

> my root is rust & red planet
> my root's hot
> my root is crossed swords

Now in my mad book I do ride,
I am King Morley of the Roads;
now in my shadow book I do slink & slip,
I am the Prince of the Sinking Ship.
Into the house the cats do creep,
O Lady of the House of Sleep.
Every street is sad, sing
nonny neighborhood no, sing hey nonny.
Mamma Mia. Cosa Nostra. Bossa Nova.

                              my root is nonny
                              my root is no
                              no no no no no

Here are some people to see you.
Good evening, Dr. Solstice.
Nurse Equinox, Bonsoir. C'mon in.
There is a serpent asleep on the sofa,
there is an eagle asleep in me.
A thousand dogs are on watch for me,
a hundred planes take off without me.
I have been warned by a man in a mirror:
"Je suis Michel de la Mort."
Pericoloso. Pericoloso. Ich habe genug.
Rivers run though my rooms.
Mamma Mia. Cosa Nostra. Bossa Nova.

                              my root is tundra
                              my root is wriggle of padlock & plank
                              my root is ladders & lizards

Now in their mad arms
they do hold me.
now in their shadow arms
I do sink.
Corporal Morley, fall in, fall in.
The cats keep bringing wings.
Every sad street without words.
Nurse, Nurse, Queen Acorn, O!
And this little Morley went

weeeeeee

        Mmmmmmaaammamaaa

weeeeeee

        root-toot-i-root!

weeeeeee

        all the way

drome.

Calm, Calm

Calm, calm, a great calm came.
Morley wanted it.
Everyone else wanted it, for him & for themselves.
And so a great calm came.

Each man has washed his house.
They have got up early,
like sailors scarlet at dawn,
& they have with mops and strange warm cloths
done their good business;
see now how the wet wood shines.

O fine green house where Morley lives,
white fur of wolf & Snow Queen
& true forest with its wind-kings of emptiness.
In such calm
drapes are drawn against great windows without sound;
and through air flies
even the broken bird,
he with the least wing. Each creature
walks shining on the ice of his life.
in the darkest wood even. The furnace

gathers to a roar in the night,
& pain flees from all portraits, even the pained
dead man on the wall is bland, the heart
has the thump of a friend in the dark.
And all in a great calm lie.

Et in Arcadia Morley

The Annual Swedish Association for the Refusal of a Hotel
requests the pleasure of Mr. Morley's pumpkin to wrinkle the
princess.

the islands between here and birth

A.A. Dariero Hudson crossed the river in a spoon. You can't
drag a horse uphill during an opera. Your poems are wigs.

the islands between here and birth

The peacocks bloom

the islands

and plant their cries

the islands

all fire.

the islands
the islands between here and birth
the islands

Able-to-Fall

(for soprano and piano)

1/ Wind, Fourth of July

Wind does one thing with clouds,
    another with leaves;
the clouds go, go, go; the leaves
    strain, but they stay.

By the time the wind
    can take the leaves
they're shattered and yellow;
    they whirl-a-whirl awhile,
then sink,
    they're the ground's.

As fast as the clouds fade,
    fresh tribes arrive;
all of the wide sky's strung
    with their traveling.

You who once knew me,
    you might think that that's
where my heart was, high.
    But these days I declare myself
on the side of the leaves,
    which, for all that the wind
can tear at them,
    stay with their trees;

though their shaking's extreme,
    though their staying's wild.

2/ Ladders Lying Down

The roof patient with me,
the rafters tolerant.

But my ladders are in love with lying down.

Rain, and such a rain.
A downpour
beyond all the laws,
descending upon the old
ovens, the mossy freezers.
And my ladders all in love with lying down.

I dreamed I stood back to back
with a wise one, felt
the heat of that healer's body.
Cold, I could not turn.

And my ladders all in love with lying down.

If wood could rust,
these are my rusty rungs.
While from the orchard I hear
low groans of the apples.
Patient with me, the harvest,
the fruit tolerant.

But my ladders are in love with lying down.

3/ Potatoes, October

Potatoes, that's what I'm after
and that's what I find
with my fork, at the first turning
seven, red ones, all sizes.
Last night's hard frost above
was just a buzz to them.

Why are the crows suddenly calling
back down the hill?
Is the spud some god
to them? They can have
these green tomatoes instead,
frozen clear through but
convincing from a distance: rare
globes of jade.

Let crows get down
on their skinny knees to these
while I help the seven spuds
make good their escape

into hot water.

4/ Meteors, August

Some spurt, some sputter,
some make a long easy arc
before they are done.
This loose fire among the fixed

we lie on our backs and wait for.
This able-to-fall,
this able-to-flame-and-be-gone.

5/ Summer

summer love you horse
summer love you harbor
summer love you meadow
summer love you stars

summer love you tides
summer love you rider
summer love you river
summer love you rose

summer love you shine
summer love you shadow
summer love you sliding
summer love you still

summer love you gate
summer love you garland
summer love you hidden
summer love you shown

summer love you fountain
summer love you flowing
summer love you slowing
summer love you still

6/ Watering

It is a timid rain, that leaves
the topsoil moist.
Go down an inch or two
and it is dust.

So you must drench and drench,
mimicking the heaven
that cannot, it seems,
leave earth alone,
as if heaven itself took form
to stand there, watering.

When is it enough?
For all you can spill,
more will appear
to be poured through you. All
the voices of the soil
require your pouring, require
such a rain
as you had not ever thought
to let fall. Many,
multiple, are the mouths
of the earth.

Can dry ground dream of rain?
What hope for the ground
without what it cannot dream of?
Then you must stand and stand
until all dreams of dust
are done, until
all you are is rain.

2

Pilgrims' Hymn
(*The Three Hermits*)

Even before we call on Your name
　　To ask You, O God,
When we seek for the words to glorify You,
　　You hear our prayer;
Unceasing love, O unceasing love,
　　Surpassing all we know.

Glory to the Father,
　　And to the Son,
And to the Holy Spirit.

Even with darkness sealing us in,
　　We breathe Your name,
And through all the days that follow so fast,
　　We trust in You;
Endless Your grace, O endless Your grace,
　　Beyond all mortal dream.

Both now and for ever,
　　And unto ages and ages,
Amen.

Song of the Driftwood
(*North Shore*)

We who were
of the air;
we whose cries
you knew;
we who flew.

Who could not bear
to leave this shore,
who chose to be here,
in these shapes,
in this other life.

To be near,
to hear
the new living cry out
as once we cried;
and the water's voices.

In the strongest storms
sometimes we stir;
no more than that.
We will not leave
this shore.

We who were
of the air;
we whose cries
you know;
we who flew.

For a Wedding
(*Canticles*)

And many loves, many old hours
are done. It is the month
that turns to the sun.

O in our gardens the shells
of so many seeds cracked
and emptied under the feeders,

and those we have fed
are flown, only the signs
of their feeding, the husks

of thousands of suns on the greening
ground. Dawn, branch, garden,
their ripe songs open. And our winter

is over.

The Church by the Sea
(*Canticles*)

"This very ancient church was used for worship by the pilgrims
who paused to rest at the adjacent hospice on their way to
Bardsey Island."

O I have been a traveler, and tired,
and now I have come
to the church by the sea.

Lambs, lambs in the fields,
white as the flowers of the sea,
and the yellow blossoms of the gorse,
scent of coconut, scent of honey.

"The corner stone . . . is not local stone and would have been
dragged for many miles until the faithful received permission
to set it up and there build a House of Prayer and Worship. . . .
Another feature of interest is the Leper's window. When the Abbot
raised the host, it is said that the Lepers stood outside by the
aperture in order to see the Blessed Sacrament."

My body I have brought here.
And miles. And miles.
Heart, heart, now lifted.

Rise up, young sun of April.
Be risen over the fields and sea.
No man, no woman, unclean.

"There were but three windows to the original building. The
congregation, being illiterate, needed no light. . . . The Belfry is of
singular style. This old bell has the ghostly habit of ringing wildly
in the night when a gale is ringing from the sea nearby."

From storms now save us.
Sailors of ocean, sailors of land.
Let us, so tossed, to harbor come.

"Any donations which the pilgrims of today can spare will be most
thankfully received. We need his prayers, too, we who worship
here throughout the year. Pray for the coming of God's kingdom."

O I have been a traveler, and wandered,
and now I have come
to the church by the sea,
to the flowers among fields
where the new lambs dream.

Bless us and bless.
Let us to harbor come.

Warrior with Shield

(*ArtSongs*)

   Henry Moore, 1953

1

As if he had crawled from the sea.

Like a son beaten down
by the dark father century or
by the mother of centuries mutilated
he sits.

He will not go back to that sea
though his bronze reminds me
of its weeds crushed inward.

It seems he could yet swivel,
that with the one good arm
and shield clipped onto muscle
he still could sweep an enemy away.
Whoever hacked him elsewhere
should step with care here.

Eyes holes. Mouth a small
starburst, as when a meteor
hurts the earth. Where halves
of the face meet, where
there should be seam—
fissure.

As if with our own hands
we might complete you.
As if you had crawled to us
for completion. As if
you were ours to grow.

2

No more
to wither in me. No more
to be made of me.

Nothing
for fathering, mothering. Done.
Caresses, none.

I have been hunted down
to my last shape. But in you,
near the echoing heart,

a silence, bear me. As I
am, as I will never be,
live with me.

Mary
(*Like Winter Waiting*)

I know that he is gentle
    Who sleeps beneath my breast,
I know he shares this silence
    Wherein we breathe and rest;
I know he dreams of meeting
    The world he soon will see,
And all the wonders of it,
    And all its cruelty.

O now I am a garden
    So sheltered and serene,
With flowers of every fragrance
    And leaves of every green;
A little one now plays there,
    It is his secret place,
And I his mother Mary,
    Transfigured by his grace.

As if a stream of starlight
    Were poured into my womb,
And skies of wandering fires
    Had chosen me for home:
This hidden sun now warms me,
    These inner stars now shine,
I carry him within me,
    I guard his heart with mine.

O I have opened to him,
    Received this tiny boy
So far within my body,
    My future and my joy;

No wind will bruise his dreaming
      Until our season's done;
How deep he sleeps, my darling,
      My savior and my son.

The Hunger
(*As a River of Light*)

"The Beloved of God." Yet I am hungry.

I could command these stones: Be bread.
They would rise before me.
I could breathe on these whitened bones,

      Haaaaaaaah   Haaaaaaah

      Flesh for a feast.
      I am his son,
      mine the power,
      the hunger.

Father in heaven,
    how could my lips be open,
how could I hope to feed,
    and any but your words enter?

Yet how high on this dry place I stand.
All these lands below me.

      The valleys,
      the rivers,
      the meadows,
      the trees.

      Sssssssssssssss

      Mine.

I could take them,
could fly from this rock,
stretch my wings.

Stretch out my wings
Haaaaaaaah   Haaaaaaaaah

Stretch my wings
out over them.
Mine the power,

the hunger.

Father in heaven,
        how do I breathe but from you?
Bare my body. Naked before you
        I kneel.

Whatever waits for me,
        whatever is to come,
I lift my head,
        I make a bowl of these hands
to receive it,
        be it water or fire
from your heaven.

Father, my source.

Consider the Lilies
(As a River of Light)

Consider the lilies;
    Solomon never,
    in all gold of his glory,
    in kingliest splendor,
stood fashioned as these.
    See the grace of their growing.

Consider the sparrows;
    what do you see there?
    Do they sow, do they harvest?
    O where are their shelters?
Their mansions of grain?
    See how God ever feeds them.

And if God feeds the birds of the air,
    and clothes the grass
    which dies in a day,
what has God in mind for you?

Consider the lilies;
    there where your wealth lies,
    you will see where your heart lives:
    all petals, all leaves.
Know the lives of the lilies.

Child's Elm Song
(*Sitting on the Porch*)

If there were no trees
I would take my turn
And stand in the street in spring
With arms wide open
In case there were birds
Who needed a place to sing.

Pebble
(*Sitting on the Porch*)

I so loved the pebble
that now leaves my hand.
I do not throw it
and it does not fly from me.
Simply, it goes.

It is as if
it is washed smooth.
My kissing
did not do this,
time did it.

Before, I put my mouth
on a landscape.
Here is a plain now,
a slighter surface.
It hums off now
to its own future,
it is like a small moon
with a painted face
that leaves me.

I think if I opened
the door of my heart a little,
a little water would run out,
not blood.
It would flow after the stone,
following it.

Bird
(*The Wife of Winter*)

A bird has come, a red
barrel-breasted puffed one
with a quick claw.
He is nimble about bread,
he is good at light loads.
O he can carry a crumb over acres,
his wings never stumbling,
he picks his way
through the flake-falling,
he lifts up into the gray
worlds of winter air
with his victory of crumb.
He will not come down to me
easily. It is his hunger only
that brings him down.

And another bird calls in the night
"No love. No love. No love"
over fields of snow.

And eagle comes to me,
as the children sleeps,
as *he* sleeps,
and we climb together over these fields;
owl senses us only, fox has a notion
in his swift, picked way through the wood.

"No love. No love. No love."

Song of the Music Master
(*The Nightingale*)

Not only is our glittering friend
Of finer structure, to my mind,
But every song from out its throat
Will match exactly, note for note,

        Exactly, note for note.

Were we to open up this bird
To seek the source of what we heard,
We should find everything in place—
The perfect musical device.

        The perfect musical device.

There is no need to tolerate
What one cannot anticipate;
Let the predictable forms of art
Reign once more within your court.

        Within your court.

3

from To Be Certain of the Dawn

"This is the task: in the darkest night to be certain of the
dawn, certain of the power to turn a curse into a blessing,
agony into a song. To know the monster's rage and, in spite
of it, proclaim to its face (even a monster will be transfigured
into an angel); to go through Hell and to continue to trust in
the goodness of God—this is the challenge and the way."

—*Abraham Joshua Heschel*

"You must teach the children, so they can remake the world."

—*Abraham Joshua Heschel*

Create in Me
(*Chorus*)

Create a great emptiness in me.
Send a wind.
Lay bare the branches.
Strip me of usual song.
Drop me like a stone,
so that I go
where a stone goes.
Send me down unknown paths,
send me into pathlessness,
into the lost places,
down into echoes
to where I hear
voices, but no words:
a place of weeping
below any of earth's waters.

Teshuvah
          Teshuvah
                    Teshuvah

Give me difficult dreams
where my skills
will not serve me.
Make bitter the wines
I have stored.
Begin the returning.

     Teshuvah.
        Teshuvah.
          Teshuvah.

Kingdom of Night
(*Chorus*)

Holy God, who find no strength in us
    to be Your power.
How should we think ourselves
    Your hands, Your feet?
How should we be Your heart?

On the day You called to us,
    in the kingdom of night
where You kept calling,
    how did we heal one another
in Your name? How did we think
    we might be recognized as You
in all we failed to do?
    In the kingdom of night
where, again and again,

out of the mouths of children,
You kept calling.

Where was the light
　　we should have been?
Moons we are, ghosts we were;
　　no way for anyone to know
that great sun shone.

And everywhere such wounds.

This we ask of You—
　　You who brought us into being—
which tasks are ours? which labors?
　　which joys? which dances?
which instruments of Yours
　　do we become?

In the time of the breaking of glass,
　　the tearing of roots,
the splitting of every little temple
　　of hope, the heart,
breathe in us, Spirit of God,
　　so that we strengthen,
so we may grow and be known
　　by our love.

Two Little Girls
　　(*Soprano, Mezzo-Soprano*)

two little girls
we are just two little girls
in the street

sisters?
what do you think?
maybe so
maybe not
maybe so

we're a little bit curious about the camera
we're not so unhappy about the camera

(who is it,
we wonder,
who is looking at us
just the two of us)

here we are

do you like the skirt?
what do you think of the coat?
pretty red coat!
it's Tuesday
so I get the coat for the day
Leah is wearing the skirt

why bread
in both my hands?
why does Leah
have nothing at all?

she has one hand
on the back of my neck
she's holding onto me
the other hand's empty

just in case
just in case

hands are for holding onto
hands are never for hurting us
hands are for giving us things

what do you think of our shoes???

Old Man, Young Man
(*Baritone*)

you can keep standing there
if you want

I'm going to stay
sitting here with my back
against this tree
and smiling to see you
just being so young

(maybe it's something
you're saying to me
I don't remember)

maybe it's because
I am father
to your mother

maybe that's not really
a smile on my face
maybe I'm half-asleep
and I'm having a dream

where I'm leaning against a tree
and Rachel's boy is standing
slender in sunlight
talking with me

I want this dream
to go on and on
and things are still good
or good enough
in this world of summer
and nothing so bad
has happened to us
not under these trees
where you stand
your back to the camera
young child of a man
young child of my child
talking with me

as if you were made of sunlight
as if you were made of leaves

Three Coats
(*Mezzo-Soprano, Tenor*)

I'm wearing three coats
or maybe it's
two jackets and a coat

I have curls hidden under
my knitted cap
am I a girl or a boy?
it doesn't matter!

(a girl)

under the coats
there's a shirt,
it's buttoned-up, too

(a boy)

and I'm wearing
a scarf
between my shirt and my vest

I just wish
it didn't hurt
where my tooth came out
didn't look so bad

and if only I wasn't
so sleepy today
(bad dreams)

and if only
father didn't look
so scared last night
when we heard
the knocking on the door

so—
a shirt
a scarf
a vest
a jacket
a coat

(I'm a boy!)
(I'm a bundled-up boy!)

Boy Reading
(Baritone)

I'm looking down
from far away
I'm high up on a branch
looking down
on the book

so many little characters
all of them keys,
says Mama,
keys to all the doors
I want to open

keys
doors
I want to open them all

I like the way
the characters are
sometimes I think I see
looks on their faces
(*they're* looking at *me*)

they'll take me
into the stories
where I want to go

I had a dream

where I grew so heavy
I fell out of the tree
down down down
into the characters

and they covered me over
and no one could find me

they never found me

Hymn to the Eternal Flame
(Children's Chorus, Soprano)

Every face is in you,
    Every voice,
Every sorrow in you,
    Every pity,
Every love, every memory,
    Woven into fire.

Every breath is in you,
    Every cry,
Every longing in you,
    Every singing,
Every hope, every healing,
    Woven into fire.

Every heart is in you,
    Every tongue,
Every trembling in you,
    Every blessing,
Every soul, every shining,
    Woven into fire.

Walking with You
(*Soloists*)

I would like to be walking with you.
    in the cool of the evening.

Walking with you
    in the streets of that city
we have imagined and dreamed.

There we are walking.

Not evening, maybe. Maybe in the heat of noon.
    Or midnight with its winds.
Not a time of our choosing.

Do not fear, I am with you.
    I will bring your offspring from the east
and from the west I will gather you.
    I will say to the north, "Give them up,"
and to the south: "Do not withhold;
    bring My sons from far away
and My daughters from the end of the earth."

Maybe a rain.
    running down the leaves,
running over the stones,
    down the roots of the trees

We are walking there.

Source of All Life,
    these eyes and faces

are You among us
as we labor to repair this world.

Maybe stars,
those faithful ones
that do not step down;
we will walk by their light,
and ask forgiveness
for smallness of dreams.

I would like to be walking with you
in the cool of the evening.
I would like to be walking
in the streets of that city
we have dreamed and imagined;
there we are walking.

Voices of Survivors

(*Soprano, Tenor, Baritone, Mezzo-Soprano*)

"I see the places, the people—they live in my memory—the faces of the people who meant so much to me."

—*Felicia Weingarten, survivor*

"Why did I survive? The Rabbi said: 'God kept you on earth to write the story.'"

—*Henry Oertelt, survivor; zl, of blessed memory*

"I dream of the sculpture of a bird—I try to touch it. I wake up touching the bird. I think it is a miracle."

—*Robert Fisch, survivor*

"I have lived in a world with no children. . . . I would never live in a world of no children again."

—Hinda Kibort, survivor; zl; of blessed memory

This work was commissioned by the Basilica of Saint Mary in Minneapolis as an offering of the Christian community to the Jewish community on the occasion of the fortieth anniversary of the Vatican document Nostra Aetate and the sixtieth anniversary of the liberation of the death camps. The four portraits (pp. 55-61) are based on photographs from the book Children of a Vanished World by Roman Vishniac.

from Considering Matthew Shepard

Keep It Away from Me

don't wanna look on this
never get near
flames too raw for me
grief too deep
keep it away from me

> *stay out of my heart*
> *stay out of my hope*

some son, somebody's pain
some child gone
child never mine
born to this trouble
don't wanna be born to this world
world where sometimes yes
world where mostly no

> *the wound of love ***

smoke round my throat
rain down my soul
no heaven lies
keep them gone
keep them never
grief too deep
pain too raw
keep them away from me

> *stay out of my heart*
> *stay out of my hope*

don't try
any old story on me

    don't even try

no wing no song
no cry no comfort ye
no wound ever mine
close up the gates of night

    the wound of love

keep it away from me

    the wound of love
    you take away
    the wounds of the world

keep it away from me

         * Gabriela Mistral

The Innocence

When I think of all times the world was ours for dreaming,
   When I think of all the times the earth seemed like our home—
Every heart alive with its own longing,
   Every future we could ever hope to hold:

    Where O where has the innocence gone?
      Where O where has it gone?
    Rains rolling down wash away my memory;
      Where O where has it gone?

When I think of all the times our laughter rang in summer,
　　When I think of all the times the rivers sang our tune—
Was there already sadness in the sunlight?
　　Some stormy story waiting to be told?

　　　　　Where O where has the innocence gone?
　　　　　Where O where has it gone?
　　　　　Rains rolling down wash away my memory,
　　　　　Where O where has it gone?

When I think of all the joys, the wonders we remember,
　　All the treasures we believed we'd never ever lose—
Too many days gone by without their meaning,
　　Too many darkened hours without their peace:

　　　　　Where O where has the innocence gone?
　　　　　Where O where has it gone?
　　　　　Vows we once swore, now it's just this letting go,
　　　　　Where O where has it gone?

Deer Song

(*Deer*)

A mist is over the mountain,
　　The stars in their meadows upon the air,
Your people are waiting below them
　　And you know there's a welcoming there.
All night I lay there beside you,
　　I cradled your pain in my care,
We move through creation together,
　　And we know there's a welcoming there.

> Welcome, welcome, sounds the song,
> Calling, calling clear;
> Always with us, evergreen heart,
> Where can we be but there?

(*Matthew*)

I'll find all the love I have hoped for,
   The home that's been calling my heart so long,
So soon I'll be cleansed in those waters,
   My fevers forever be gone;
Where else on earth but these waters?
   No more, no more to be torn;
My own ones, my dearest, are waiting,
   And I'll weep to be where I belong.

> Welcome, welcome, sounds the song,
> Calling, calling near;
> Always with me, evergreen heart,
> Where can I be but here?

We Are

we are all sons of fathers and mothers
we are all sons

singing

we are all rivers
the roar of waters
what is the world to us?
who can we be for the world?

there is a star at morning and one at evening
they are no more the names we give them
than we are

everything singing beyond itself
beyond the names we love (O love) to give them

everything swelling beyond its powers
everything lifted up in the singing

we are sparks that scatter through the world
from original fire we come

we are the flow of sky and its unfolding
we are hundreds of hoofbeats on hard ground

sometimes no home for us on the earth
no place to lay our heads

if you could know for one moment
how it is to stand in our bodies
within the world

you ask too much of us
you ask too little

everything brimming in us
everything dark in its barrel

we are
            be
we are
                become

we are

            bless

we are

               dream

we are all sons

singing

Even in This Rain

signs of You everywhere, signs in the darkness
signs in the fires
signs of You in the hurt streets
signs in the tents, the tunnels
signs of You in the tiniest beating heart
thank you our cry to be sung

even in this rain

out of the mouths of visions torn open
out of abandoned tongues
out of the mouths of children lost in the furnaces
out of the bloody lullabies
out of the beaks of buried eagles
the forests wrapped in rags
wires of lightning loose and writhing
out of skies as stained as the seas
we cry our song to be sung

even in this rain

sit with her now, old earth
hear her stories
all we have already been given
all we have yet to do
on watch
keeping our hands in the wounds

even in this rain

how might we ever say to You
we have ceased to dream
never forgetting
remembering how every breathing remembers
to build the world
thank you our cry to be sung

nobody
      no one
            turned away
nobody
      no one
            unworthy
nobody
      no one
            ashamed

yes each silence
yes each radiance
yes each shadow
yes each praise

mind into heart, mind into heart
each dream walks on

even in this rain

thank you

All of Us

What could be the song?
   Where begin again?
Who could meet us there?
   Where might we begin?
From the shadows climb,
   Rise to sing again;
Where could be the joy?
   How do we begin?

Never our despair,
   Never the least of us,
Never turn away,
   Never hide our face;
Ordinary boy,
   Only all of us,
Free us from our fear,
   Only all of us.

What could be the song?
   Where begin again?
Who could meet us there?
   Where might we begin?
From the shadows climb,
   Rise to sing again;
Where could be the joy?
   How do we begin?

Never our despair,
　　Never the least of us,
Never turn away,
　　Never hide our face;
Ordinary boy,
　　Only all of us,
Free us from our fear,
　　Only all of us.

Only in the Love,
　　Love that lifts us up,
Clear from out the heart
　　From the mountain's side,
Come creation come,
　　Strong as any stream;
How can we let go? How can we forgive?
　　How can we be dream?

Out of heaven, rain,
　　Rain to wash us free;
Rivers flowing on,
　　Ever to the sea;
Bind up every wound,
　　Every cause to grieve;
Always to forgive
　　Only to believe.

Most noble Light, Creation's face,
　　How should we live but joined in you,
Remain within your saving grace
　　Through all we say and do?
And know we are the Love that moves
　　The sun and all the stars, *

O Love that dwells, O Love that burns
    In every human heart.

(Only in the Love, Love that lifts us up!)

This evergreen, this heart, this soul,
    Now moves us to remake our world,
Reminds us how we are to be
    Your people born to dream;
How old this joy, how strong this call,
    To sing your radiant care
With every voice, in cloudless hope
    Of our belonging here.

Only in the Love,
    Only all of us . . .

(Heaven: wash me . . .)

All of us, only all of us.

What could be the song?
    Where do we begin?
Only in the Love,
    Love that lifts us up,
All.

* Dante

4

Song for Joey

O I can sell you a talking plum
I can sell you a squeaking rose
I can hire you a horse as thin as your thumb
        But you'll have to pay through the nose, the nose
        O you'll have to pay through the nose

O I can give you a grinning fish
I can give you an apple that snows
I can find you a king who is fit for a dish
        But you'll have to pay through the nose, the nose
        O you'll have to pay through the nose

O floating foxes, O squirrels that sneeze
O world that nobody knows
O I can give you whatever you please
        But you'll have to pay through the nose, the nose
        O you'll have to pay through the nose

Doctor Livingston

I took the dog for a walk in the park
There were snakes on the swings
There were goats in a tree
As we were rolling and running along
A camel came up and spoke to me:

> Doctor Livingston, I presume
> Diddledy Daddledy Doddledy Doo!

I went to the grocery store on the corner
Bought mustard and roses
Bought wine and baloney
As we were floating and fluttering home
I heard from the bag the Voice of Baloney:

> Doctor Livingston, I presume
> Diddledy Daddledy Doddledy Doo!

I love the rain
I love the snow
I love the street
I love the neighbors
My table is red
My ceiling is blue
My dog's vegetarian
How about you?

I wrote to my mother who lives underwater
I wrote to my brother
Who lives in a cloud
As we were wobbling and waddling back
The mailbox followed us, shouting out loud:

Doctor Livingston, I presume
Diddledy Daddledy Doddledy Doo!

I am the sun
I am the moon
I am a man
I'm marmalade too
My dog goes Miao
My cat goes Moo

Doctor Livingston, Doctor Livingston
Diddledy Daddledy Doddledy Doo!

State Fair Song

I want to learn to sleep
like the pigs at the State Fair;
oh, how those swine could sleep!
Teach me! Teach me!

Like princes
in palaces
of straw

        Snore ... Snore ...

there they lay,

Like hairy
like milky
kings
slumped on their thrones

        Snore ... Snore ...

there they lay.

How do you do it, hogs?
The secret, the secret!
Snort me your secret
from the barns of sleep,
O swine!
Teach me! Teach me!

        Snore ...
                Snore ...
                    Snore ...

Tree of Two Birds

Tree of two birds,
tree of two birds,
all winter long
I have heard your song,
and my heart has been like
a tree of two birds.

When it was cold, cold, cold,
when the snow flew,
when the clouds rode
down
                down
                          down

such song
from the bare branch—
sweet throat, sweet throat,
all winter long.

Even the darkest days
how you plant
your notes in my heart;
like a fountain,
green fountain in winter,
fountain of my friends,
like my family
singing to me,
O Brother
O Sister
bird
from the twigs of winter.

Tree of two birds,
tree of two birds,
feeding me with your song
all winter long.

Chickadee

Chickadee—
don't be afraid of me!
I am the one who feeds you—
Chick-chick-chickadee!

Here I am, come here!
A scarecrow with fat hands
of corn and sunflower seeds—
Come and feed from me!

Let all birds comes, all kinds.
I can buy, I can buy
good seeds for you all winter long,
O tiny tribes!

Friends of the air, don't be
afraid of the coming cold;
like a magic man in the fall
I'll put out corn-seed

and at solstice sunflower,
flowers of the sun.
Chick-chick-chickadee—
you can rely on me!

Singalo Singalay

Sing me a song like the morning,
Sing me a song like the rising sun;
　　Simple and flowing,
　　Tender and growing,
Sing me a song for everyone.

Singalo, Singalay,
　　Follow the call of our melody,
Singalo, Singalay,
　　Join us in the joy of harmony.

Bring me a song like the river,
Bring me a song like the summer stream,
　　Soothing and shining,
　　Gentle and twining,
Bring me a song we all can dream.

Singalo, Singalay,
　　Follow the call of our melody,
Singalo, Singalay,
　　Join us in the joy of harmony.

Only the sounds of our singing,
Round upon round ringing everywhere,
　　Laughing and playing,
　　Dancing and swaying,
Show us all the life the world can share.

Singalo, Singalay,
　　Follow the call of our melody,
Singalo, Singalay,
　　Join us in the joy of harmony.

(*Harmoonia*; a children's opera)

Really Silly

You're a bed, you're a head
    With a said made of soak,
You're a roast in a rose
    With a nose made of most,
You're a sloop in a slip,
    You're a really silly swip,
You're a beef in a belfry
    And you're boast boast boast,
You're a beef in a belfry
    And you're boast.

You're a leg, you're a keg
    With a peg made of pout,
You're a winch in a wok
    With a mock made of munch,
You're a well in a will,
    You're a really silly sill,
You're a log in eleven
    And you're lunch lunch lunch,
You're a log in eleven
    And you're lunch.

You're a clamp, you're a champ
    With a lamp made of loot,
You're a sink in a sack
    With a whack made of wink,
You're a peak in a puck,
    You're a really silly luck,
You're a cheer in a cherry
    And you're chink chink chink,
You're a cheer in a cherry
    And you're chink.

The Pink Flamingo Motel Song

The Pink Flamingo is a nice motel,
The Pink Flamingo is a nice motel,
The Pink Flamingo is a nice motel,
Fly, motel, fly.

I tell my pillow I must go to sleep,
I tell my pillow I must go to sleep,
I tell my pillow I must go to sleep,
Bye, pillow, bye.

The rooms are neat,
The beds are strong,
The dreams you have
Will last you all night long,
There's lots of hot water
And some cold stuff, too,
Yes, it's just the place
For me and you, you, you, you:

The Pink Flamingo is a nice motel,
The Pink Flamingo is a nice motel,
The Pink Flamingo is a nice motel,
Fly, motel, fly
                        Mingo, Mingo,
Fly, motel, fly,
                        Mingo, Mingo,
Fly, motel, fly!

A Song for Children Possibly

O never shake hands with snow
Unless it invites you first
Once I made a mistake
With a horrible flake
And it wasn't the flake came off worst

O never take tea with an apple
Unless you are sure it is wise
He may be a bore
Or bruised to the core
Or a serpent in subtle disguise

O never go swimming in April
For April is terribly deep
Be sure that you know
How to bellow and blow
Or to bleat like a bee in his sleep

O never dance tangos with rhinos
Although they may seem very sweet
They simply can't sing
Or do anything
And those b*st*rds will ruin your feet

The Last Day of May

The sky on the last day of May
Has never before looked this way;
It's wide and it's blue
And reminds me of you
When you've something amazing to say.

The cuckoo the last day of May
Has something he's trying to say:
He starts: A . . . B . . . C . . .
And then: Oh, yes . . . D . . .
But he never can get all the way.

The robin the last day of May
Has several blue eggs tucked away:
She thinks it is best
Just to sit on her nest
And plan a vacation—Olé!

My Uncle

My uncle lives in an acorn,
He likes to live that way;
    When I hear a breeze
    In the tops of the trees
I see my uncle sway.

Up my uncle into the clouds
And down my uncle again;
    When he smells the snow
    On the branches below
He rolls his eyes in the rain.

Give Her the River

(for soprano and trio)

If I could give her anything,
  anything at all
in all of the world
  to show how I love her,
I'd give her the river.

Give her the river at dawn,
  when it shines,
when the swans are gliding.

Give her the way the willows
  lean,
how they sway
  in the green of their dreams.

Give her the swallows
  that flicker flicker flicker
over the river their home.

Give her the old stone steps
  leading down to the river
and the little blue wildflowers
  that are starting to grow there.

Give her the fresh shiny leaves
  of the oaks and elms,
make her a May basket
  from their fluttery shadows.

Give her that line of geese
  headed upstream;
they're honking so hard
  I think they think

they're pulling that boat
  behind them.

Give her the way
  the soft deep water slides
like sleepy us sometimes
  after reading and reading.

Give her that small wooden bench
  where we can sit and watch
the river do all the work
  for a while.

Give her the tinkle of the bell
  on that Scottie's collar
and the grin of the Scottie's owner
  as they jog by.

Give her that one white cloud
  in all the blue sky—
my girl will find some game
  to play with it.

Give her the river at evening,
  we'll smile
at the first of her stars.

Give her the heron
  floating over alone,
and the moon,
  Queen of Herons,
behind her.

Give her the quiet canoe
   that gleams
like a piece of moon.

Give her her very own
   dream of the river
where she sails with friends
   all summer
till she comes to the sea.

Give her the last of the light,
   silvery, silvery,
little waves, little leaves
   little scales, little gleams.

Her river.

5

The Road Home

Tell me where is the road
    I can call my own,
That I left, that I lost,
    So long ago?
All these years I have wandered,
    O when will I know
There's a way, there's a road
    That will lead me home?

After wind, after rain,
    When the dark is done,
As I wake from a dream
    In the gold of day,
Through the air there's a calling
    From far away,
There's a voice I can hear
    That will lead me home.

Rise up, follow me,
    Come away, is the call,
With the love in your heart
    As the only song;
There is no such beauty
    As where you belong;
Rise up, follow me,
    I will lead you home.

Hymn for America

We have loved you for your rivers,
    We have loved you for your shores;
Every treasure you have shown us,
    Every seed that you have sown;
We have loved you for your mountains,
    For your prairies, for your fields,
All these gifts we have been given,
    All these glories that we share;
Now we thank you for these blessings,
    We, your people, everywhere.

Many are the stars of heaven,
    Many are the hopes of earth;
All around us, worlds unfolding,
    All around these dreams to grow.
From the moment of our rising
    Till we rest when day is done,
May we tell our hearts' own story,
    Hearts that honor and believe,
Through our care for one another,
    For this life and land we love.

Carol of the Hill

On my ground
    With a crown of thorn,
He died for us
    Who for us was born;
The tree that flowered
    Is cold and bare,
No songs, no singing
    Anywhere.

            O Bethlehem,
                Ah, Jerusalem.
            Ah, Jerusalem.

Second Adam,
    Son of Man,
Into my earth
    Your life's blood ran;
Now from this earth
    New trees will grow
With fruit, with flowers,
    I swear it so.

            O Bethlehem
                Ah, Jerusalem
            Ah, Jerusalem

For you I shall wear
    A crown of trees,
And birds shall sing
    From among your leaves
For you I shall wear

A crown of trees,
Now sing, birds, sing
From among your leaves.

O Bethlehem
Ah, Jerusalem
Ah, Jerusalem

Hymn for Dad

on your journey
to the river
we are walking
walking with you

light around us
light within us
calling, chanting
humming, singing

sway of summer
leaves of laughter
O my sister
O my brother

one in mind
and one in grace
and one in heart
and one in spirit

all we need
and ever near us
mercy shining
always on us

light around us
light within us
we are walking
walking with you

on your journey
to the river

Song of Gratitude

Out of this love, out of this longing,
    Out of these voices from all of the ages,
Out of these songs, out of this singing,
    Lifting our souls, lifting our being:
Heart, you are everywhere,
    Deeper than dreaming;
In the name of the spirit of love,
    Always and everywhere,
We bow down, we bow down:
    Namaste.

Within the source, within the center,
    Within the telling of falling and rising,
Within the root, within creation,
    Harvest of waves, dancing redeeming:
Hope, you flow everywhere,
    Healing our wounding;
In the name of the spirit of love,
    Always and everywhere,
We bow down, we bow down:
    Namaste

Harmony flesh, harmony treasure,
    Harmony human, forever returning,
Harmony path, harmony vision,
    Blessing our way, endless beginnings:
Light, you shine everywhere,
    Leading our wonder;
In the name of the spirit of love,
    Always and everywhere,
We bow down, we bow down:
    Namaste.

The Holding Carol

All the days feel like winter
    Filled with shadows and gray
Eyes are heavy, spirits drifting
    Seems it's always that way

For a young child, close beside me
    I longed to sing from my heart
'Bout a light that I can see
    *Shines in me, shines in you ** *

Yes, you are like a starry sky
    Yes, all the leaves of every tree
Yes, you are all the sweetest songs
    Heard in the heart

Dream, let us always always dream
    Dream how the world can ever be
Dream every blessing we receive
    Deep within this joy

Here we are, breathing peace
    In this holy place
Every longing we have known
    Mercy and grace

This is the healing
    Gently flowing in us
Only joy, only joy
    Here we are
Here we are

Yes, you are like a starry sky
    (You have always been)

Yes, all the names of every flower
    Petals floating free

Dream, let us always always dream
    Dream how this life can ever be
Dream every blessing we can share
    So deep in this love

Holding us, holding us,
    Love is always holding us
No more fear in the blessing
    Of resting in You

We are Yours, Yours only
    Here we belong
In this dark, in this light
    World You have made

Only this, how we are together
    Silent, silent
Only this, Heaven that we know
    Heaven we feel

Only Love all about us now
    Only Love that lives within
Love rivering in us
    Love walking with us still

This world Love has made
    Where we are.

* Craig Hella Johnson

Song from the Road

Long on this journey
    Long in these shadows
Far from the only home
    Low all our hoping
Deep the undoing
    Just the forsaken road

Voices we dream of
    Echoes remember
We all together there
    Heaven was once
Our song to be singing
    Hearts' every word
In wonder and joy

> *I am how your heart discovers*
> *All the hopes that sleep in you*
> *I am every silence calling*
> *I am Fountain   I am Meadow*
> *I am every secret door*

> *Sing your ships into their harbors*
> *Sing them bring them heal them home*
> *Murmur every holy river*
> *I am Harvest   I am Blossom*
> *I am leaves around your soul*

Come from the shadows, into the gleaming,
    Dawn of the day in us;
Open our lives to everything growing—
    How shall we breathe this grace?
World we are watching, world we are,
    Keep us in life with you.

How do we answer? How do we know?
　　Love bring us closer. Mercy us home.

　　　　I am how your heart discovers
　　　　All the hopes that sleep in you
　　　　I am every silence calling
　　　　I am Fountain　　I am Meadow
　　　　I am every secret door

　　　　Sing your ships into their harbors
　　　　Sing them bring them heal them home
　　　　Murmur every holy river
　　　　I am Harvest　　I am Blossom
　　　　I am leaves around your soul

Carol of the Stranger

Peace and grace be to this house
    Where all are welcomed in;
Receive the guest, receive this heart:
    Tell the Stranger, tell.

> *Tell the Stranger what you cannot tell*
> *Those who love you and desire your joy;*
> *Tell.*

Make tall your walls, make long these beams,
    Who once believed alone;
Make wide the circle, feed the fire:
    Tell the Silence, tell.

> *Tell the Silence what you cannot tell*
> *Those who love you and desire your joy;*
> *Tell.*

Blessings be upon this place,
    Let every wound be healed,
Every secret, every dream:
    Tell the Angel, tell.

> *Tell the Angel what you cannot tell*
> *Those who love you and desire your joy;*
> *Tell.*

Peace and grace be to this house,
    All will be returned;
Let every soul be called your own,
    Tell the Mystery, tell.

> *Tell the Mystery what you long to tell*
> *Those who love you and desire your joy;*
> *Tell.*

A Blessing of Cranes

How do we love you more than to shape you?
Turning so quietly within the shadows of fingers.
How do we love you more than to let you go?

Waves of earth's oceans, waves of our willing hands
Creasing and folding, creasing and folding, unfolding.
How do we love you more than to shape you?

Never a thought of thinking, only this weaving,
These thousands of wings we make to carry our longing;
How do we love you more than to let you go?

No trembling before the task, simply this sweetness,
Freedom from fear, receiving this heartbeat, receiving.
How do we love you more than to shape you?

Blossoms that shimmer and gather about their branches,
Returning to earth her peace, her original blessing;
How do we love you more than to let you go?

Deeper than dream to say, even than singing,
Releasing the wishes we have, the asking for healing;
How do we ever love you more than to shape you?
How do we love you more than to let you go?

Senbazuru *is a group of one thousand origami paper cranes held together by strings. A Japanese legend tells that anyone who folds a thousand origami cranes will be granted a wish by a crane. The crane in Japan is a mystical or holy creature said to live for a thousand years: that is why a thousand cranes are made, one for each year. In some stories, it is believed that the thousand cranes must be completed within one year and they must all be made by the person who is to make the wish at the end.*

Little Heart of Ages

Little heart of ages,
    Spirit child,
Heavenly our dreamer,
    Here you lie;
Light is all about you,
    Petal now eternal,
Little heart of ages,
    Spirit child.

Every lamb is yours, Lord,
    Every one,
Leaping out of time now
    To the sun;
Never was a soul born
    That was not a treasure;
Every lamb is yours, Lord,
    Every one.

Blessings to the children
    On this day,
Blessing to all pilgrims
    On their way;
Glory to the light
    That leads us to the kingdom,
Welcome to the children
    On their way.

Light upon the Water

Like the light upon the water,
    Summer in the swaying tree,
Radiance of the woken flower,
    You are these and more to me.

From this hour, from this moment,
    Where we make our holy vow,
No more distant, no more hidden,
    We are undivided now.

Life before us, love within us
    More than we can sing or say,
Everything is grace, is given,
    All our dreams begin this day.

Credo Noli Timere

We know we belong to You.
When we lose heart, when we despair,
Whenever we tremble,
                         tremble
                                        tremble,
It means we have forgotten You.

Bring us home with every breath,
With every beat of the heart
We in You and You in us,
And remember
                         remember
                                        remember
The freedom of our belonging to You.

All flesh comes to You
All the beautiful names are in You
All rivers and veins and sinews of the sea
All languages, all silences
All leaves and flames and blossoms and rains and wings
All voices we have ever longed to hear

Help us to know ourselves
    always worthy of Your love
                         credo alpha, omega
To know how we deserve Your joy in us
                         credo corazon
Help us to heal our world's divided houses
                         credo sangha
Help us restore and bless and release
                         credo sunyata
Lead us from the real to the unreal
                         Abwoon d'bwashmaya

May we sing out in every holy tongue
                    credo neshamah
And freed from every fear
                    credo noli timere
                           noli timere
                                  noli timere
May we be Your mouth
May we be Your music

                    homage to Seamus Heaney

Joseph

"I was like a father holding you in my arms"
—Book of Hosea

a starry sky is in my arms

I hear my breathing—now not only mine
each dawn is different now that you are here

sometimes I stare at you, sometimes I tremble
I stand above you, my head a moon
and you down there on the sweet straw

each dawn is different now that you are here
I hear my breathing, now not only mine

all my dreams for you, wondering
who you might be, how far you may have come
to be with us

each dawn is different now that you are here

sometimes I feel among waves too steep,
my boat too small
for these wide hands to have made

when I've been working, when the sun is low,
I sink into the stream and lie there, pale as stone
and still this burning that I feel
so deep inside me

how are you mine, child?
how are you ever mine?

I am like a father
I am like a father

so let the old Joseph die, the new be born
hold high this lantern for the world to see—
this child, this light, this saving one

a starry sky within my arms (O heart)
each dawn is different now that you are here

Kin

you are all my kin

in the small hours
I claim you

set out in your shadow boats
by sail by paddle by oar

we'll meet
on a vastness of water

however wild it may be

all of you my kin
and I claim you

From Heaven Above to Earth You Come

The Earth before You came to be
    Was never such a place as this,
So filled with Holy Mystery;
    The Earth before You came to be.

You come to lead us all to You
    Who lay upon the simple straw
With creatures breathing by Your side;
    You come to lead us all to You.

Within each heart You make Your home;
    We once were hungry, now we feed;
You open every life to love;
    Within each heart You make Your home.

We once were shadow, now we shine;
    All pilgrims on the path of light.
O kingdom come, we call Your Name;
    We once were shadows, now we shine.

Our joy to be what You have dreamed,
    Von Himmel hoch, das komm' ich her, *
Our joy to know this grace you share,
    Ich bring euch gute neue Mär;
O more than human voice can tell,
    Der guten Mär bring ich so viel;
Our joy to be what You have dreamed,
    Davon ich singen und sagen will.

* *Martin Luther*

Leaves Are My Flowers Now

Leaves are my flowers now.
Basswood and sumac,
their banners and flags,
aspen and oak,
their shreds, their ribbons, their rags,
flutter and rattle.
Leaves are my flowers now.

Now is most fruit
shrunk to husk,
petal to small skull;
now are most things
gone from air,
now I see no dragonfly
out over water,
nor butterfly, with high sails
of yellow and black,
more beautiful than may be,
nor wasp, whom frosts
have silvered and slowed.
Now is light expert
among them, takes first
this pulse, then this one,
now shines a little
this surface, now
stains, now prescribes.

Clearer and clearer
the paths I pick.
Basswood and sumac,
their banners and flags,
their shreds, their ribbons, their rags,
flutter and rattle.
September is almost over,
and leaves are my flowers now.

"wanted to be an artist"

wanted to be a fireman
wanted to be a nurse
wanted to be a dancer

hold that flame steady within your hands
    if a wind comes, turn
to where there's no fear for the flame,
    the flame's survival

live as you can with these long shadows
    if you fall into the surrounding reservoirs
swim as imperceptibly as you can
    over the dark water

wanted to be leaves
wanted to be waves, wings, warm feathers
wanted to be what stays

shimmering on the canvas
after the brushes have moved on

for the children and parents of Newtown
12/22/12

North Star Song

How long have you been watching
    While we became below
Enough of what we're dreaming
    To come to call you home?
How long have you been shining,
    So high and unafraid,
Upon the roads we've traveled down,
    The choices we have made?

Before we had our meadows,
    Our cabins and our towns,
Before we harnessed rivers
    Or felt this land our own,
While eagles circled over,
    While sun and moon sailed by,
You never faltered, only kept
    Your faith upon the sky.

The streets we walk together,
    The lives we guard and feed,
The harvests that we gather in,
    The visions that we need—
This blessing we are sharing,
    This bounty that we hold,
The gold of sun on water,
    The gleam of moon on snow.

Let nothing narrow keep us
    From all we treasure here,
The call of songs and stories,
    That echo through the air;

However we have come here,
  How many lives we are,
We keep the watch, we stand like you,
  Our north, our home, our star.

Now We Belong

Here are the voices of every creature,
    Here are the calls of every heart;
Here is the place of strangers' welcome,
    We who once walked in strangers' shoes.
Once we were strangers,
    We were welcomed,
Now we belong and believe in this land.

Here are the rivers of many echoes,
    Here are the leaves of every tree;
Within us live the long horizons,
    Winds that stir the sacred stones.
Once we were strangers,
    We were welcomed,
Now we belong and believe in this land.

> *Keep faith, keep watch,*
> *Take heart, take courage,*
> *Guard mind, guard spirit.*
> *Feed love, feed longing.*

Here are the cities where we have gathered,
    Here are the barns where hope is stored;
We are the gleams of every being,
    Filled with the dreams that build the day.
Once we were strangers,
    We were welcomed,
Now we belong and believe in this land.

> *Keep faith,*
>   *Guard mind,*
> *Take heart,*
>   *Guard spirit,*

Take courage,
  Keep watch.
Feed longing,
  Feed love.

The Unfolding: a Ruah Prayer

(*for women's voices*)

When were You ever not
    our Mother?
When were Your wings ever not
    in us?

      O Thou   *O Thou*
          Ruah   *Ruah*

As once You moved over the face
    of the waters,
even so we feel Your flowing,
    Your flowing through us.

        Ruah   *Ruah*

Our sister You are,
    our Always,
our Neverendingness.
    As wheat gleaming, so we
should dream.

      O Thou   *O Thou*
          Ruah   *Ruah*

In the night You are with us,
    nearer than near.
How should we fear?
    You will not let the heart
be lost, be lost, be lost
    in the shadows.
O Thou
    O Thou
O Thou

          Ruah
                    Ruah
Ruah

With every folding, unfolding,
    folding, unfolding,
all waves of the world,
    all worlds of Your making
within us, revealed.

O Thou   O Thou
          O Thou
                    Veni   Veni
O Thou   O Thou
          O Thou
                    Holy   Healing
Ruah   Ruah   Ruah
                    Veni   Veni
O Thou   O Thou
          O Thou

                    in memory of my sisters

122

With Every Song

How do we tell You, how profess
    These blessings we receive from You?
Longing be lifted by all tongues;
    How shall we praise You save with song?

When we grow wearied on the road,
    When shadows fall and spirits fail,
Be with us as we journey on;
    How we have loved You is our song.

We are Your people of the Word,
    Joyfully gathered in Your name;
Help us remember we belong,
    O strengthen us with every song.

to the melody of the "Old One Hundredth"

Thanksgiving Grace

Bless this table
Bless this company
Bless those before us
Bless those to come

Help our humanity
Steer our uncertainty
Bring us to wisdom
Bring us to love

for the McLean Family

Voice Lesson

in memory of Krista Sandstrom, singer

all the years are a voice lesson
there is so much to sing
we need every instrument

so we may sound the depths
of where we are, how we are
ever to know one another

no lanterns of moons I know
to send across the evening sky
other than music

no petals to set in procession
upon the breathing stream
save our songs

all the years a voice lesson
there is so much to sing
we need every instrument

The Voices

*for Dale Warland and the singers on the occasion of their farewell
concert, May 30, 2004*

I don't know if we have ever deserved
    the voices, but they are ours,
I don't know if we ever have known
    what it means to be able to speak
in those tongues, and only
    in my worst, most useless moments
have I tried to imagine
    our lives without them.
Where might we go in the world
    where they would not reach us?

I would never go into the dark
    without the voices,
I have come to rely on how they mend us
    among the ruins
of what we have hoped for.
    If there were only one branch in the world,
the voices would find it.

Doubt was never the root of us,
    doubt winds itself, again and again,
around our doing,
    but it was never the source,
joy is the source,
    foliage of joy in which
the singers are hidden, but heard;
    always the gate, always the garden,
always the light, the shadows,
    always the leaves.

From where I stand now,
    I cannot see every singer,

but looking out across the years,
    listening in ways learned
only from them,
    I can hear all the song.

6

The Now, the Long Ago

In the dream time of the swarming snow
We're on the couch, just chatting, you and I,
Here in the now, there in the long ago.

The world outside is singular and slow,
As if the winter taught all things to sigh
In the dream time of the swarming snow.

I'll make our supper, then we'll watch a show,
And then you'll choose some stories, by and by,
Here in the now, there in the long ago.

So many things that you don't need to know
About the years, the years that simplify
In the dream time of the swarming snow.

This won't go on forever, child, although
I've never had the words to tell you why,
Here in the now, there in the long ago,

Won't be for always, little love, and so
We'll take this all as blessing, you and I,
In the dream time of the swarming snow,
Here in the now, there in the long ago.

Evensong

"There he is" he learns to say
when we glimpse the great sun burning down
toward the hill, and "There she is"
when we spot the pale enormous moon
floating low above the pines;
and over and over, swiveling his head,
he says it as I drive them both,
daughter and son, around the roads
until they sleep, so I can have
dinner and an hour alone with their mother.

Ahead in the shadows, two deer.
A little further, metal abandoned
in somebody's yard, auto parts
and ancient appliances, that later
the moon will make into something,
that same skilled stranger keeping us
company beyond the branches.

He wants to know why they share the sky,
and all I can tell him is it's a secret
we have to guess at as we go;
and "There he is" he says once more
as the hill prepares to swallow fire,
and "There she is" as she climbs the air,
and murmurs and murmurs until he sleeps
(and she already is sleeping).

August Hymn

We do not tire of dreams you bring,
    Of ageless rumors often told,
Or all these years of love for you,
    Your tales, your parables.

We kneel amid your harvest gold.
    We see your stillness in the day,
We feel your tremblings in the dark,
    Your leaves, your mysteries.

We bow before your silences,
    We know that they have heard before
What we are murmuring to them,
    Your stars, your dragonflies.

We want no other earth than this,
    This everywhere of holiness,
While all about the kingdom sway
    Your rains, your promises.

Carol of the Sailor

Taking me, taking me,
    Ship through the water,
Taking me, taking
    To harbor, to home.
There is a child
    My eyes must see,
There is a kingdom
    To which I must come.

        Blow winds,
        Harder, you winds.
        Riding the hills of the sea!

Bringing me, bringing me
    Quick through the currents,
Bringing me, bringing,
    Swelling the sail.
There is an evergreen
    Grows in our winter,
There is a new one
    To whom I must kneel.

        Blow winds,
        Harder, you winds.
        Riding the hills of the sea!

Coming now, coming now
    Into his starlight,
Entering, entering
    Out of all storms.

Let me hold in my arms
    This youngest of seabirds,
Let me lift, let me rock
    This small boat in my arms.

        Blow winds,
        Harder, you winds.
        Riding the hills of the sea!

Prodigal

"We are on fire because our souls come from beyond"
—Plato

Walking through all the dreams to be there.
The miles, the dust, the winds, the rains, the shadows.
Keeping on, careful
not to fall out of the world.

At last the path, the flowers, the fragrances,
the wings, the singing, murmurings
of all the hidden lives. At last
the door, at last to open, to enter.

Here where you once held me,
I see you always, the eyes, the smiles.
You did not wait till dark to light your lamps.

Each door in me now swung wide,
each trembling window shining.

Melody

Blind Melody now brought to your door.

She must be with you for a while;
tell no one of this guest you hold.

You will know when she must leave
when you yourself can see no longer,

and only with her gone can you begin
the singing which was once against

your will, your power, your dream,
but is now your meaning.

Song

Playing tennis in the snow
With my true love, most gladly I

Did let her win each game, each set.
I praised her grave, inaccurate eye

And proudly as she leaped the net
Did raise her in that world of snow

And sing the song all lovers know:
Six Love, Six Love, do such games go.

Seven Last Voices

in response to The Seven Last Words of Our Savior on the Cross
by Franz Josef Haydn

1/ House

"Father, forgive them, for they know not what they do"
"Pater, dimitte illis; non enim sciunt quid faciunt"

You are descending stairs—
    down and down and down.
Slowly, as in dream.
    You have never wanted to go this deep,
but the House of Forgiveness is large.

As if you were among the roots of oaks.
    Up there, storms;
you know the branches grind and shriek,
    but here no groaning, only this quietness,
as of whales asleep.

Is this down here the dream?
    Or is it up there, where you do
things as wild as, wilder than,
    those plunging branches?

All hates, little and large, that you hold,
    let those winds sweep them from you,
send them as leaves down the street,
    let *these* deeps murmur to you,
wary of them as you were
    (and now their salt
washing your wounds clean).

Forgiveness—has she lived here all along?
    Out of her blood once you came,

and so soon you hissed away from her,
    from whose body you began by drinking
before you learned any words
    to distance yourself from her.

And why such a stranger here?
    Why have you lived away?
Why only a guest in these rooms?
    Descending now, breathing this darker air;
what is to be done
    other than watch and listen
out of the heart she gave you?

Now windows are being opened,
    you feel it everywhere,
and what is this fragrance
    all through the air?
It is forgiveness.
    Forgiveness and her flowers.

2/ Thief

> *"This day you will be with me in paradise"*
> *"Hodie mecum eris in paradiso."*

At least they did not cut off my hands
    and leave me helpless.
At least they have only killed me,

Where you go, now I go.
    You said: come with me,
you shall be with me.

You said: I know the paths.
So: I will follow you.

All I know is that we die
        here together.
All I can do is trust you,
        tied as I am beside you.

My own crimes, I know.
        Too many, too often.
What was yours?
        Was there the one only?
A large one?
        (They seem to have made
larger wounds in you.)

At dawn light this morning—
        it was so cold, remember?—
I did not know that now
        I would be walking these paths with you.
Are we near water?
        I think I see boats,
hear what sounds like ropes,
        slapping against masts
within a harbor.

This going with you,
        I already love.

As a boy,
        I never knew the names of trees,
but these are cedars.

3/ Mother

"Woman, behold your son."
"Mulier, ecce filius tuus."

I thought I *had* my son in this life.
    And now, you give me another.

When did you ever not surprise me?
    It was not always an amazement
I would have chosen,
    but each time, like a dream, it was there
and I belonged to it.

Do I hold *this* one to my heart?
    Is that what I must do?

As if forgiveness were not already enough,
    already so much,
now this?

Was there ever a time you did not ask of me
    more than I thought I could do?
I have never dreamed myself as large
    as you presume me to be.
Really, there are only so many rooms.

You never let me live my only life;
    you never did.

But in all you have asked of me,
    I did not fail you and I will not now,

even now, though this is hardest,
    here in this place where you suffer so.
When I said yes—long ago—
    to be your mother—
I was young, young—
    how could I have known
what this would ask of me?
    And could this be the last asking,
as you die before me?

I hardly think so.

I never knew how much
    could break in me,
and still be green.

And now you say, my son:
    Behold your son.
You cannot ask it, and you do.

Here I am.

4/ Tsunami

> *"My God, My God, why have You abandoned me?*
> *"Eli, Eli, lamma sabacthani?"*

The sea has taken everything. What has the sea *not* taken?

The sun looks like a scar, the birds like scars in the branches—
where there is any kind of tree.

Why is there nothing? (The something, as it just was,

was never so much.)
Why is there now nothing?

Why is there another day after this one? Then another, then
another?

What are the nights for? Yet I prefer the sky dark, so I never
expect a sun.
I prefer the poor light of stars.

Dark, or light, there is nothing left to dream.

My God, My God, I cannot begin to ask what You were thinking.
I cannot begin to dare to imagine that You might have turned away
just a moment from the world, even that You were beginning
to think of a different world, wearying of this one . . .

I cannot believe that for even a moment You drew back Your heart
from us.
Why, then, *this heartlessness?*

We have been betrayed not only by the sea, but especially the sea.
Everything we had broken; everything known.

Lord, You, even You, even if You are there in some lost corner of
my heart, calling like a mad bird, I do not hear You. Instead *I* call
and call.

Am I still Your bird, even if I am a mad one?

My God, My God, I always knew You were with us. Now do I
know?

Mother, mother of my mother, mothers, can you tell me anything beyond my own question with its thousand mouths: Why?

When I was a child, always they told me there was light, that the light was real, but was hidden. And now?

Hidden is beating its drum, its drum, its drum.

5/ Line

> *"I thirst"*
> *"Sitio"*

I do not know how long the line is. I know I am not the first of the thirsty, not the last. The line goes round the world.

Cracked the lips of the children, the lips of the mothers, the lips of the fathers.

The belly is a begging bowl, a shallow little thing. It trembles, but we are not to see that. (Only surgeons, like ravens high above the body, could look down and in.)

These are lives in which rain has not fallen for years: no slow steady soaking of rain in the night, no loosened earth, no fragrance, no flowers unfolding, no silky lotus with its leaves unfurled.

Lord, now that we know You thirst, what is our own dryness but Yours? Yours but ours? You thirst, since You are with us, even till the end of time, Your bowl no bigger. With us in this line.

Did you tremble in Your own abandonment? I have imagined Your
wounds so wide that small animals ran there to hide from the
hunters—nothing You could do about it, nothing You would have
chosen to do, even if Your hands had not been nailed to wood.

No creature too small for You to be its savior, to take upon
Yourself its thirst.

The line goes round the world. Your world.

6/ Over

> *"It is finished"*
> *"Consummatum est."*

Apples. Olives. Table. Door. Dust. Rain.

It is over.

The whale in her deeps. The hawk, circling.

Scar. Cut. Bruise. Vein. Pulse. Bone.

Over.

Mud. Straw. Coins. Dawn. Twigs. Wind.

Your mother's songs. Your father's stories. Games with the little
friends.

Over.

The sheep with their bells. The goats—of course the goats.

Hands. Lips. Bread. Fingers. Tears. Healing.

It is over. Pockets emptied of minutes and hours and days.

Mercy, the oil.
Mercy, the womb.
Mercy, the breath.

Over.

Now go to Mercy herself.
The One who always strengthened You.
The One in whom there was nothing You could not do.

Waves rolling onto the shore, sliding away.

It is over. It begins.
It is over. It begins.

Riddles. Blessings. Teachings. Streams. Leaves. Birds.
(Maybe the birds go with You.)

Now, how can we not know what must die in us?
What must grow less?
What lives?

It is over. It begins.
It is over. It begins.

It is over. It begins.

7/ Pantokrator

"Father, into Your hands I let go my spirit."
"In manus tuas, Domine, commendo spiritum meum"

What did not begin with You?
What goes back to You has always been with You—
   in Your hands, we say, but *not that, not that,*
      we know You are Spirit, that there are no hands,
      and when were we ever not in them?

How do we return to You?
   Ground of our being (*not that, not that*),
     Ruler of All (*not that, not that*)
       though *Father*, we can say, though *Mother*,
        since from the first breath
        we have loved those names.

In our need, in our joy, we have spoken to You,
   little intimate conversations,
     Who knew us since before we were born.
      Nothing we would not say to You
       Who know all the rivers we are.
        Nothing in us that does not flow to You.

Into Your hands, though Your hands are the sky,
   into Your heart, though Your heart is all flowers . . .
     See, we cannot imagine You!
      And *since* we cannot imagine You—
       Immensity, forgive us, then.

With what does not die,
   with what in us does not know how to die,

we come.
    Like children,
        like leaves before the wind.
            Father. Mother. To You.

Words for Music

Writing words for music is like building a boat rather than a house—you want something firm, buoyant, that will float when the music arrives. Build too heavy, and things sink. (And most words for music on the page are as about as interesting as boats on sand.)

You leave room for the music. The main job of any text written for music, poetry or prose, is to release the composer's shaping spirit—the words, like those of a poem on the page, being an opportunity for their reader (in this case, the composer) to imagine. Working with words, I start by pulling structures, some of them very free indeed, from out of my own world of shapes, and offer them toward the music. This involves huge amounts of play, lots of eventually unusable material—if it occurs to me, I write it down—until, at usually some late stage in the process, a vision of order begins to suggest itself. At that point, I am drawing upon patterns from anywhere that may be of help—from what I love and know in poetry, prose, painting, music, landscape, and the like—until at last the work is, if not finished, at least ready to show to the composer. Then come, typically, discussions, revisions, re-revisions, bargainings, dismemberments even. The text for music is always provisional.

I have no idea how "my" composers do what they do and have often been astonished what they have been able to make out of the sometimes very informal possibilities I have proposed to them. Recitative-like language can become, by some miracle of art and craft, aria-like music; gleaming veins of musical formality can appear in verse I had thought was, in essence, "free."

On occasion, the music comes first—the roles are reversed and a whole other set of challenges comes into play. This is a relatively rare circumstance, but some of my favorite experiences have been when I set out to try to find some words worthy of an outstanding melody—for Stephen Paulus' "Pilgrims' Hymn," for example, or "As a River of Light" by John Foley S.J. While I'm likely to tremble at such a challenge, I also relish the opportunity—I bring everything I have in me to bear on the task.

And it is in such situations—when something formal, such as a repeated melody with metrically identical stanzas, tends to be involved—that I get closest to my favorite forms of music, the hymn and the carol—the latter generally the pre-modern kind, as in "Lullay My Liking, My Dear One, My Sweeting" . . . "There Comes a Ship A-Sailing" . . . "I Sing of a Maiden That is Makeless" . . . "Balulalow," and to write words which, though not pastiche, are my own form of reverence toward the spirit of those sprightly, tender sounds. As a non-musician, I also enter into a deep kind of connection with my long-dead father, my organist, choirmaster, pianist, singer, English father, whom still, though I am now older than he was able to be, I hunger after.

Then there is the matter of harmony, that magical simultaneity of effect for which composers are, quite rightly, the envy of verbal artists (for all Ezra Pound's talk of the image as a "visual chord"). In the presence of harmony, I find my appetite for life, my inclination to *make something*, enhanced to an unusual degree. "From harmony, from heavenly harmony, this universal frame began," writes John Dryden. I believe it.

I'm not sure how guilty a pleasure this is, if it is one at all; I take courage, as it were, from D. H. Lawrence's vivid essay "Hymns in a Man's Life" or Elizabeth Bishop's choice of seven hymns as "poetry of a kind, I am fairly sure," in the fall 1994 issue of the Academy of American Poets' *Poetry Pilot*, and it can be revealing to trace the influence on certain very free-spirited, free-form poets of some very formal and traditional sources—of Blake on Allen Ginsberg, say, or Chaucer on Philip Levine.

One large difference between words of poems and words written for music is the size of the audience involved. As a librettist, from the start I am not "someone alone in a room with the English language," as Berryman describes the poet; rather, I am part of a team, not my own boss, something of a second fiddle—and I relish (that's that word again) the happily subordinate role.

And when—to take one example—"Pilgrims' Hymn" was sung at Orchestra Hall in Minneapolis in 2001 at the "Elegy" concert commemorating the tragedies of September 11, sung by a combined choir of three hundred voices, to an audience of perhaps two thousand and, beyond them, to a national radio audience, I was very aware that in the service of music, words of mine can reach many more people—unprecedented numbers of them—than those my books of poems, with their very modest visibility, are able to. Stephen and I have the sense that this hymn has truly entered the repertory and is finding its way into people's lives in the way that only music—even only songs of a certain kind—can do. (It is not a matter of sales and statistics, of course, but of a different kind of belonging.)

How do I feel about this? And how do I feel about these boats of mine, this "poetry of a kind," as Bishop calls it? Well, I feel lucky, for one thing, lucky beyond any deserving, for the company and friendship of the composers I have worked with, and for what I have learned in the many dialogues that our collaborations have involved. The writing I have done for musical performance I see as worthy, overall, and in harmony with the writing I have done for the page (though it is always my hope that the poems will be taken off the page and heard as speech, the most musical speech I can manage). While there are only a very few pieces I have written for music that I might ever recite at a reading *as poetry*, I view them all with a certain fondness as, to use Plato's term, my "mental children" (though some of them live very far away now and don't get back to me too often). To have been able to contribute in this way, so that the words, married to the music they were written for, are sung in churches, temples, concert halls, school gymnasiums, studios—and may, some of them, be sung for even a considerable time to come—is more privilege and luck than I could ever have hoped for when I first set out on my life as a writer.

In my most recent collaboration with Stephen Paulus, earlier this year, I was asked to come up with words for an exquisitely touching melody, "Prospect," from the *Southern Harmony* collection of 1835, for which Stephen had been commissioned by Dale Warland to create a new arrangement. After first talking with Stephen about the overall mood of the piece, and some possible themes, I lived with the melody for several weeks, singing it to myself over and over, trying out many phrases and combinations of phrases, cutting and pasting and discarding, and had several further lively, detailed discussions with Stephen, usually about drafts I had sent or brought to him, both of us (writing partners, on and off, since 1976) working to achieve the significant simplicity we felt this music required.

Here are the words we came to for the third and final verse of "The Road Home," sung, in performance, in four-part harmony with a solo soprano descant in the third verse:

> Rise up, follow me,
>> Come away, is the call,
> With the love in your heart
>> As the only song;
> There is no such beauty
>> As where you belong:
> Rise up, follow me,
>> I will lead you home.

You would not hear this from me at a poetry reading, but it's a great tune, and I love to sing it.

2001